EDEN *miniatures*

ENCOUNTERS

Optimist

Encounters

Ponderage

There are, I come to realise, an infinite number of infinities.

When I put this to my young Mathematician Friend as a question, he interprets it mathematically and gives me an explanation I do not comprehend, but of which I have a faint feeling it appertains to something entirely different, though nonetheless relevant and important. Maybe I did not phrase my question well, and he did not understand it. Or very possibly he did fully understand the question and gave me a perfectly valid answer, but one that makes sense to his young mathematician mind more than it does to mine, which is twice as old and really not scientific at all.

I have enjoyed my young Mathematician Friend's company, and I miss him and think of him often. He has a lovely smile, though it be slightly downward inclined, which makes him look just a tad sceptical when he smiles. Then again, he is a mathematician, so he has every right to be sceptical, and his smile is no less lovely for it.

I am fairly convinced that since there are more infinities than just one, there may well be several, and if there are several, there may well be many, and if there are many, then conceptually it strikes me as obvious that most likely there are an infinite number of infinites. Not being a mathematician, or at all scientifically minded, I only know of three infinities, two of which are of the same kind, and a third that is of an entirely different kind.

The reason I know that there are more infinities than just one is that there is the infinity of rational numbers, which perch on the unending line in the plus/minus direction where you can always add one more or take one more away. This means you in a sense already have two infinites, a positive and a negative one, but they are, in character, the same and should therefore probably be considered, if not one, then of one ilk.

But there are also the irrational numbers, which, like anchor points or switches on that line stretching from negative infinity into positive infinity, branch off into another direction, or even dimension, by leading into the unending sequence of never repeating numerals after the decimal point, which we can't simply add to or take away from, but have to calculate, and which is therefore specific but unpredictable, but predictably unending.

So, simply looking at these two types of infinity, which are easy enough to understand though they may not be instantly recognisable, my hunch is chances are there are perhaps—I would venture quite probably, so probable as to seem certain—other infinities that may be even less easy to recognise, but that are nonetheless real, as real as these two (which could be looked on as three); and so, since there are an infinite number of numbers and an infinite number of ways we can configure these numbers to express an infinite number of things, there are likely, I like to think, to the level of this being probable, and in fact quite possibly so probable as to seem certain, not just two, or three or four, or one or two dozen, but an infinite number of infinities, not least

because there are bound to be an infinite
number of universes.

The thought that there are an infinite
number of infinities to me is beautiful
because I like the idea of infinities, but it
is also tiring, because while I can imagine
the one or two infinities that I'm already
familiar with, I can barely conceive of any
beyond that; and right now I wish I could
have my young Mathematician Friend with
me and curl up with him, just to feel his
calm body in the presence of his beautiful
mind and know that there is someone
who may not see the world quite as I do,
but who can handle abstraction and make
something of it.

We spend some time together at the
Science Museum, and on my terrace,
and in my bed, and then he goes back
to Austria, where he's from; and I think,

this is true: we actually met on a park bench in Kensington Gardens. It feels like we've known each other for years, but we really just met last Thursday by the Italian Fountain, when he asked me for a light, and we talked and exchanged numbers.

I lost sight, a little, of my young Mathematician Friend, after he left London, but he didn't entirely escape from my mind, and so we met up again a few months later, this time in Vienna. That was a little strange, because now a few things had happened—none of them to do with me—that had troubled this beautiful mind of his, and while he was better again, in fact well, I now worried about him, and we talked about all manner of things, but not infinities. And then we spent a whole night together, first going out, drinking many pints of stout in an Irish pub, and then at a nice little hotel, and I thought no more

of or about it, until it occurred to me that
this, probably, is what most of life is mostly
about: chance encounters, and where we
take them, if anywhere at all.

We didn't take our encounter much
further, my Mathematician Friend and
I, but that matters not; what matters
is merely that we made ourselves some
memories on a pin prick of an infinite
number of possibilities, and for that alone I
like him still.

Alignment

Here is how the universe aligned itself for it to happen that my young Science Communicator Friend and I could have a wonderful night, with Morcheeba:

I'd had every intention of going to the Highlands for a few days in the last week of November, firstly because I love the Highlands and like to go there sometimes in the autumn when there are not many people about, and there's a good chance of rain, and the walks are solitary and long, but also, secondly, I had an offer of a free first class ticket from King's Cross to Edinburgh courtesy of East Coast Rail, which was about to expire in early December: a gift of 'goodwill' from the train operator by way of compensation for some long service delays the year before.

I was pretty much sold on the idea of doing this because I craved the craggy hillsides, and I thought on the way back I could drop in on an old friend in Berwick-upon-Tweed and go for one or two more walks with him before Christmas, and for once I was not strapped for cash. So, so far so good.

The First Thing that went wrong, as in right, as in different to all expectations and most precedent, was that my old friend in Berwick was going to be 'on duty' that particular weekend—the last one in November—because his wife was going to take herself off somewhere with the oldest, leaving him home alone with the two smaller children. This put a clanking big spanner into all kinds of works, since it meant that far from being able to go on extensive country walks followed by many pints in the pub, we would have to spend time mainly at home, looking after said small children. Now, they are lovely children, but that was not what I'd had in mind.

The Second Thing that offered itself up as a variation on the 'plan' was that a dinner that had been suggested a while ago by the Swiss Ambassador and His Wife for a small group of people including me was now scheduled for Thursday 27th, and although I had very mixed feelings about the circumstances in which this invitation came about—for reasons that would be inappropriate for me to enter into in anything resembling detail—I actually rather liked the Ambassador and His Wife and thought that it would be churlish or at the very least ill mannered to miss their dinner, in the absence of any good excuse for doing so (other than my lingering unease about what had precipitated the occasion in the first place, of which more I am honour-bound not to divulge).

My enthusiasm for the prospect of spending the end of a Highland week at my friend's in Berwick already dampened, I thus now also had an almost perfectly good reason to stay in London that week and accept this invitation, signalling to the Ambassador and His Wife that, certainly on my part (I couldn't speak for the other people concerned) there were no 'hard feelings,' and so all was, comparatively speaking, well...

Now newly in a position of having this whole week mostly to myself in London, I started filling in some other nights in my diary. Though not the way they turned out at all, because the Third Thing that happened was that I was having coffee with

TomTom at the Troubadour. There was no reason or purpose to this, he just happened to be in London with a break near the end of his tour and suggested we go for coffee, which I, being a creature of habit and feeling at home at the Troubadour, suggested we do there.

At some point Anders, the lovely lanky waiter of Scandinavian origin whom I have never not had a bit of a soft spot for (bearing in mind though that I tend to have a bit of a soft spot for waiters generally, especially tall ones), came over and handed me a blank envelope. This had never happened before. It was, he said, an invitation to a private view of a local artist, Melinda, who had asked him to give some of these to some Troubadour regulars, of which clearly I'm one. Pleased and a little flattered, I thanked him, slid the envelope in my pocket and proceeded to more or less forget about it in an instant.

When I got home after saying goodbye to Tom, I found the envelope in my jacket and put it down together with my unopened mail of the last few days, possibly weeks, there to forget about it for a second time. (There was no noteworthy reason why I had at least several days'—possibly several weeks'—worth of unopened mail: I just don't like opening my mail. Nobody these days writes me poetic epistles or missives of undying love: what comes through the letterbox are mainly bills, unsavoury bank and credit card statements, and 'special offers' that have nothing special about them from companies I have little or no interested in.)

Meanwhile, around about the same time, on the 18th November, to be precise, so actually a couple of days before having coffee with TomTom, I was trying to organise a night out with Diego, who is not only adorable as well as Italian, but also difficult to pin down socially, because while he's extremely loyal and helpful, he's also unfeasibly busy. It's a typically 'London' challenge, this, which we're all used to.

I had proposed two films to him (as an alternative to the theatre, simply because he hadn't yet responded to my other suggestion, which had been *Electra* at the Old Vic), and while he was keen to see the film on Turing, he had in fact already arranged to see *Interstellar*, my other option, with some other friends in the very near future. Reasoning that as an Italian he wouldn't mind, I blithely invited myself along, asking him specifics about the date and time he had booked, which turned out to be Friday night 28th at seven forty-five.

I went online straight away and found one
of very few seats—mainly singletons left
to the side and very front or extreme rear
of the IMAX auditorium—and booked it,
triumphantly announcing to Diego that
I was going to crash his night out at the
cinema with his friends.

Also on the 18th November, I start a
conversation with a man on Grindr. He
describes himself as 'masculine looking for
the same, but love a good chat regardless'
and looks like a handsome, slightly rugged
early thirty-something to me. He is on his
way home, past my house, it appears, after a
failed encounter with a 'weird' Italian—no
connection to my Italian friend—who has
spooked him a bit; and while we're both
online he reaches his flat, which happens to
be eight doors precisely along from mine,
on the same side of the street. We chat a
while longer, find out that we share several

interests and are both night owls, until finally I sign off because 'I'm starting to fall off my perch,' as I tell him, some time after three in the morning.

The next day we chat again, briefly, then we skip a day, and then over the next two days (we're now up to 22nd November) we again have just a few brief exchanges on the app, except I tell him that curiosity has got the better of me and I've entered his name in the search field on Facebook, and the first person to come up was him. I offer to send him a friend request, which he suggests I do, and we banter a bit about possibly finding out too much about each other and 'the joys of online stalking.'

So from the 22nd November he and I are friends on Facebook. This is the Saturday before the week I was going to go to

Scotland, but now won't be. Nothing else noteworthy happens over the weekend.

On Monday 24th—and we're now into the week in question—JayJay, more or less out of the blue, and also perhaps a tad surprisingly since we had only just seen each other a couple of times in a row when often we go without catching up for months, suggests I join him and some friends at a tiny North London fringe theatre to see a piece either by or adapted from Gogol. I have no pronounced interest in either the piece or the venue, but I'll go and see anything more or less any time, and I am again pleased and a little flattered to have been asked, and so of course I say yes.

The night at the theatre is Wednesday, which tangentially reminds me that I have an invitation also to a private viewing at the Troubadour on that evening, but naturally

JayJay and the theatre take precedence
over a local artist whom I don't know, nor
have ever heard of, and so as I confirm
with JayJay, I prepare to forget about the
invitation I received through Anders at the
Troubadour for a third time.

Tuesday all is quiet and nothing unusual
occurs.

Then, on Wednesday 26th, the Fourth
Thing flicks a new switch, retroactively:
my friend David reposts an item of his
girlfriend Alex's on Facebook, in which she
offers two tickets to see Morcheeba this
coming Friday. The reason the tickets have
become available is that she had bought
them mistaking the date of the gig for the
previous Friday, so she had rolled up at
the Shepherd's Bush Empire then, only
to be told that she was a week early. This
coming Friday she can't do. (Whether she

was going to see Morcheeba with my friend who is her boyfriend, David, or somebody else, I don't know.)

I respond to David's forwarded post, saying that I have use for one ticket, so if any of his other friends also has use for one, then we could have ourselves a night out with Morcheeba 'tomorrow.' This is a slip of the mind, as the tickets are actually for the day after tomorrow, but I don't notice that. I do, however, look up my diary correctly for Friday, because in the diary for Thursday is the Ambassador and His Wife's dinner, and on Friday there is nothing.

This is the Fifth Thing, and it's decidedly odd: I have three Apple devices, which are all using the latest, up-to-date operating systems, and which ordinarily synch all my diary entries across devices via iCloud, so I pretty much trust my diary. Since my diary is blank on Friday, I think I can go and see Morcheeba then – the fact that I talk in my reply to David's forwarded post about 'tomorrow,' when tomorrow would be Thursday, turns out to be a red herring.

But my diary isn't free on Friday. I have a ticket booked, crashing Diego's cinema-going party at the IMAX. Yet this doesn't show on the laptop I'm using. Later I find out that the diary entry exists, perfectly accurate, on my other laptop. When I notice this and run several tests to see whether my diary isn't synching properly, I find that there is no such issue, my diary synchs wonderfully, within seconds; and if a device happens to be offline (I test this too), the entry gets pushed through at the earliest possible moment, no problem. So why, of all my diary entries, this particular one did not come up on my laptop at this time, is and remains an unsolved mystery.

At almost exactly the same time, the Sixth Thing that happens is that JayJay texts me to say that he's feeling poorly and won't be making it to the theatre tonight. I read this as a cancellation of the outing as a whole, since I don't know his colleagues or friends and had left it to him to book the tickets. So I think: no worries, I will go to this art viewing instead. Also at the same time approximately, my new friend from Grindr gets in touch again for the first time since the weekend, this time on Facebook, with the opening gambit: "so we're facebook friends now."

Having previously mentioned the Troubadour and the possibility of a coffee there in our earlier chats on Grindr, I take the opportunity, offered by the Sixth Thing, to tell him that I'll be heading down there later today and that there'll be free vodka cocktails, a fact which Anders had alerted me to from the start, and which had stuck in my mind as a particularly attractive incentive, because how can you say no to a vodka cocktail when it's on offer. To my absolute delight, my new friend says he could do with a free drink and agrees to come down and see me there, exactly as I'd hoped, because that would give us a chance to meet really informally in a relaxed setting, and it would only have to last half an hour if it didn't go well. He has promised his flatmates he would cook some chicken soup for them beforehand, so we agree to meet down there at seven, which gives me a chance to also have some chicken soup beforehand, though I didn't make mine from scratch, I poured mine out of a Waitrose tub.

The art at the viewing is decorative and nice with quite a bit of character, and as

I'm there before my friend arrives, I chat a short while to the artist, who thinks she knows me, but when I tell her that we don't know each other, although she may have seen me at the Troubadour, she seems to lose interest and becomes almost a bit weary, though not impolite, notwithstanding the fact that I also tell her, of course, that I had been invited by Anders.

The vodka cocktails on offer are Sea Breezes, generously poured by Hugo (I think – I'm never entirely sure if his name is Oscar or Hugo or something else entirely), and I find two elderly ladies who are locals and friends of the artist's to chat to while holding out for my friend who's since messaged to say he's running a tad late.

By half past I tell him that I'm more or less done with the art now, but he says he's just on his way, so I take advantage of my two elderly ladies hanging around near the entrance talking to an attractive and artistic looking woman whom I estimate to be around halfway between my age and theirs, and I effectively crash their conversation, which leads to me and that very attractive and somewhat artistic woman talking to each other—me facing the open door—as my friend bounds up the stairs. I recognise him instantly from his picture, and we greet each other like we've always known each other, which in a way I feel we have.

I introduce him to the attractive woman, whose name I can't now remember though it may have been Yvonne, and he, realising that I'm mid-conversation and aware that he's very late, proposes to find himself a drink; I ask him to bring me one too and continue talking to 'Yvonne' until she reckons it's time to look in on her sixteen year old at home, and since my friend has not got back yet with or without drinks, I go looking for him to see if he's all right.

I am massively pleased to find him talking to another random gallery-goer, though for reasons that don't strike me as obvious, but not important enough to enquire about either, he hasn't got me a drink, he's only picked up one for himself, so I get me my second one too, and I join them.

For the second time, I feel like I'm here *with* him, of course, who else: although we only now really speak our first few sentences to each other, we may as well, for the level of familiarity I feel, have been together for years. And I say 'together' here, even though we're not even friends yet, and it is absolutely clear to me even now that we we may never, in that sense, or any other, be 'together.'

The woman he has been talking to eventually makes her way off too, and we're finally left to speak to each other, which doesn't change anything; we have one more drink each, and although I feel tempted to eke out another, he is attuned to the fact that the place is emptying out and suggests we make our way home as well. As we get to his front door, we embrace and nearly give each other a peck on the cheek but not quite, and I go home thinking, well that was just entirely perfect.

I'm home shortly after nine, where I find David has replied to my post in response to his post on Facebook with: "You must have a friend seb or just crack a grinder one out! Haha."

Now, as I'm about to explain to my brand new friend in a new message on Facebook, I've never been one not to "take a random gag as a proper suggestion," and so I offer the Morcheeba night out to him. It's a long shot in every sense: it's at just two days' notice, we've only ever had a couple of drinks together and hardly actually spoken to each other, and it's Morcheeba, who create a wonderful sound but who are something of a throwback to the nineties. But once again he surprises me in the best possible way and says, yes, he loves Morcheeba, he's up for it. I tell David, David promises he'll email the tickets. Everything is hunky, except...

The next morning—Thursday—I wake up with a mildly suspicious feeling that I may have messed up a bit. I check my diary and that's when I find out about the synching issue. I resolve, of course, to stick with the new arrangement and blow out Diego, simply because he's already got several people to be going to the cinema with, whereas I've now promised to take David's girlfriend Alex's Morcheeba tickets off her, and of course I can get to see that film any time.

In the evening, I go to the dinner the Ambassador and His Wife are hosting at their residence, and it is very civil, even friendly. Of the small group who had been invited, two or three had decided they were busy elsewhere, so it feels even more intimate than it would have done if everyone had attended, and as the evening draws to its close, the Ambassador's Wife again thanks us all for all we have done for the Swiss Embassy over the last few years and hands us each a bottle of champagne as a final gesture of conciliation and appreciation.

Friday comes, and there's a Seventh Thing. Having effectively written off my booked ticket for *Interstellar* at the BFI IMAX, I do feel it's a shame that that should just go to waste, especially as it's a sold out screening. So I look up my email confirmation, on which of course it says "no refunds and no ticket exchange," but I phone up the cinema anyway and say to the charming man who answers the phone, 'I realise this is not your policy, but seeing that you have a full house I wonder is there any chance you can resell my ticket?' Without dropping a beat he says: 'You can't make it tonight?' I confirm, no, I can't. 'I'll refund your ticket for you straight away, would that help you enormously?' – 'Yes, that would help me enormously, thanks!'

I'm wondering is it a coincidence, or have I manipulated my memory, or is it just the beauty of the universe that it has aligned Seven Things so my new friend, who I'm about to learn is a science communicator, and I could have a wonderful time with Morcheeba. After the gig we go for another drink, and after that we pass by my door now, coming from this direction, and I don't even have to really ask, we both just go up together, and because it was partly the Ambassador's Wife who was to blame for the fact that I didn't go up to Scotland, I crack open the bottle of fizz she gave me at the dinner the night before.

It tastes all the more lovely for everything that has brought us to this moment right here and right now.

{Vignette}

At the Servant Jazz Quarters cocktail bar, the bar lady dressed in wide black and white stripes fixes me with eyes not unkind but commanding attention:

'Do you think,' she asks me, her eyebrows like raven's wings arching high above the cliffs of her teeth: 'that people are afraid to love?'

'Yes,' say I, without hesitation, for I know I am.

'Why?' she shoots at me as if I had made it so.

'I don't know.' And it's true: I don't know, but I think that maybe it's because it makes us feel vulnerable, and I say so: 'Maybe because it makes them feel vulnerable.' (I change the pronoun, hoping that she won't notice.)

'And is that a bad thing?' she demands, probably having noticed, and I say it isn't, but it's what makes us afraid. (I hadn't really ever given it much thought. Coming to think of it, I hadn't given it any thought, really, ever.)

I feel I may have short-circuited the conversation by closing the loop with my answer, and maybe she feels so too as she places a Death in Venice in front of me on the bar.

Why are we afraid to love?

Reprise

My Science Communicator Friend takes me right back. Back to when everything was different and new and a little bit daunting, but also, obviously, exciting. He is up for things, he's up for seeing some local art on a spur of the moment, he's up for hearing Morcheeba, he's even up for a book launch next Tuesday, though that is now unlikely to happen as he seems to have mistaken Thursday for Tuesday and realised he needs Tuesday to cram for a deadline Wednesday morning. Either that, or whateverthiscouldbecome has got stuck in its tracks now and shuddered to a sudden but not in its entirety incomprehensible halt.

When I say 'whateverthiscouldbecome,' I should first of all quickly check back with the reality I am currently vaguely familiar with. The last time we saw each other, there was a moment that went like this:

We've arrived at the Shepherd's Bush Empire, and the place is as yet fairly empty, with only a couple of dozen people or so huddling near the very front, by the stage, so we are able to get ourselves a couple of drinks and leisurely hang about the part of the stalls that will soon fill up with gig-goers, standing.

I don't remember what prompts the question, but it comes mid-conversation, as an aside, almost, or a sub-clause, certainly not a big deal, when he asks me how old I think he is. It's a question in parentheses (a by-the-way kind of question that may or may not have slipped into another, much more pertinent topic of conversation) and I say, 'well, putting together the information

I have, I think you're probably a bit
younger than you look'—bearing in mind
I originally thought he looked comfortable
in his very early thirties—'so I'd say
possibly mid towards late twenties, about
twenty-seven?'

'Yes, I am twenty-two.'

In view of this, any notion of
'whateverthiscouldbecome' acquires its
very own peculiar kind of perspective.

It takes me right back, all of this, to when
things were new and a little bewildering,
but also mostly handled with aplomb.
There was a period—I'm not sure where it
started, where it ended or, if not ended, was
left dangling, suspended—when we faced
each day with a healthy nonchalance. For
me, it wasn't my twenties. I went through
my twenties with extreme caution and an
at times crippling level of self-deprecation,

but even then a tingling sense of thrill that anything at all might happen (even if very little happened, or nothing at all) was more or less always there. It was there now, with my very young Science Communicator Friend who had agreed to see me again, but then cancelled, but then—*yeay!*—agreed to, and did, see me again...

Shakespearean Lunch No 3

The first three Shakespearean lunches take place at almost exactly monthly intervals in April, May and June. The first two more or less set the tone, but they still don't entirely prepare me, for the third.

The first one happens at a beautiful Spanish tapas place just by the entrance to Borough Market, and—like all of them—is scheduled to last for about an hour, maybe an hour and a half, starting at one, but I don't remember leaving before four, maybe four thirty. Still, there is much to talk about—writing, crowdfunding, and, of course, Shakespeare—and so my stupendous Writer Friend and I take our time and order another bottle of wine, but eventually we decide to have done, mainly really because the place, beautiful as it is, isn't entirely cheap, and both of us are effectively skint.

For the second one, the tapas place is full up, and it's raining off and on, and so we head a few doors into the market to a nice fish restaurant, which is all covered in glass and lends a view onto Southwark Cathedral. Much as on the first occasion, we meet at one, and we talk about writing, a little less about crowdfunding, a little more about adventures with agents, and about Shakespeare, a lot. I have another drink to go to that evening, so reluctantly, somewhat painfully, I drag myself away shortly after six.

For our third Shakespearean lunch we are fortunate in that a small outside table is available back at the tapas place on the corner, and my excellent Writer Friend is already parked there by the time I arrive.

I have recently written a play about
Shakespeare and his relationship with
the recipient of his 'Fair Youth' sonnets,
and my friend is researching a story about
William Shakespeare's brother Edmund,
so on this occasion our conversation for
obvious reasons focuses almost exclusively
on Shakespeare. Not having strictly learnt
my lesson from our previous lunches, one
and two, I have once again brazenly booked
another drink on the Southbank at seven,
but with a friend who has stood me up so
many times and has so frequently been so
unreliable that I think not too much of it
when, around about seven, we just really
have nowhere near exhausted our topic and
order another bottle of wine.

It is at around this time that our luncheon
turns epic. There is a fine line between an
ordinary writerly lunch, which can easily

last five or six hours, and a lunch that turns
into something memorable, noteworthy.
This is approximately the point at which
that happens, because at approximately
this point we have, between the two of us,
had between four and five bottles of wine,
and in all seriousness our conversation is
likely by now to have drifted off said topic
somewhat. I don't remember onto what.
I am pretty certain my formidable Writer
Friend doesn't either, though I haven't
asked him.

I feel a little reluctant to ask him what he
remembers of our third Shakespearean
lunch, because I would not for one
moment wish to embarrass him or make
him feel uncomfortable. Not that there
really is much reason for either of us to
feel embarrassed or uncomfortable, save
for the fact perhaps that we first pay our
bill at five thirty, but when we finally say

goodnight to each other some time close
to eleven, another bill for wine has been
clocked up and paid for, and I have given
up any attempt at catching up with my
other friend, two or three increasingly
incoherent text messages having failed
to establish where exactly he was, or why
exactly he wasn't, as I suggested, simply
joining us, ten minutes' walk from where
we had arranged to meet on the Southbank
nearby.

But there's also one bottle of wine that's
unaccounted for. At some point after the
second bill, we must have decided to have
just that one more, and our brains at that
late stage of our lunch were no longer, it
seems, capable of placing paying for it into
the category of 'things to do before leaving.'

Not that we were trying to do a runner.
When I phone the restaurant the next day,

on my first attempt there is nobody there to take payment for the bottle, but they say they will phone me back. When they don't phone me back, I try again, and this time round a *Maître'd* who doesn't seem in a particularly appreciative mood recalls: 'Yes, you paid for the first ones, and then you kept hugging the guy, and then you were gone.' He is still for some reason unable to take payment over the phone, but promises to call me back, for certain. For a second time, nobody calls me, so I accept that last bottle as a drink on the house and consider the matter dealt with: thank you, it was much appreciated.

But when he says: 'you were hugging the guy,' he is, I think, being diplomatic. Or is the term I'm looking for 'euphemistic.' I am fairly certain that by the time we finally staggered to our feet we were effectively snogging. This is slightly unusual and

also unexpected behaviour from both
of us because we're just mates. Also, my
affectionate Writer Friend as far as I know
has never yet been gay. Then again, it
doesn't really matter whether or not anyone
is or isn't, and I don't hold with these labels
in the first place, and so I really don't have
any concerns about this, at all.

Still, the image that I couldn't have seen
at the time, but that is now ingrained on
my imagination, cheers me no end: the
two of us, men in our no longer quite
forties, winding up our lunch at a Spanish
tapas place in Borough, at close to eleven
o'clock at night, cuddling and kissing with
really, by that time, not a care in the world,
and still so much to talk about for, I would
hope, many a Shakespearean lunch yet to
come...

{Threesomes}

The conundrum of the three bed hotel
room.

Every standard business hotel seems to
have them. I don't get to stay in business
hotels that often since I rarely 'do business'
as such, but occasionally somebody needs
me to be somewhere, and they put me up
at a hotel, and while it's normal for the
room I stay in to just be an ordinary double
bedroom with an ordinary king or queen
size bed, every so often—probably because
all the ordinary double bedrooms are
booked—they put me in a three bed room,
and my mind fairly boggles: it's practically
never a room with three single beds, it's
usually a room with a not very big double
bed and a single bed.

Who stays in these rooms, and how? What do they *do* there? I try to imagine the scenario, but it doesn't stay salubrious for very long, and then I take a step back, and I try not to imagine the scenario, but instead the moment somebody says to themselves: well, there are three of us anyway, why don't we share a room.

Who are these three people? Are they parents and their one, lone and lonely child? That would make some sort of sense, if the child weren't very small any more, so it wouldn't be better off in a cot, but not yet grown up enough to want to stay in a room of their own. But why stay in an ugly business hotel if you're a family of three? Why not go to a nice seaside or mountaintop hotel, or a charming B&B? Maybe they're visiting the grandparents in this particular city, but the grandparents' house isn't big enough to put them all up. But that surely can't account for the number of these three bed rooms in these standard business hotels?

Who else travels in threes? Probably not the managers, that seems unlikely. The more lowly personnel who are expected to share rooms, like the sales people? But then how do they do this: do two of them share the double bed, and one sad creature has to sleep alone in the single bed, hugging a pillow? How do they choose who gets to sleep with whom? Do they rotate, if they're there for more than one night? Are they there for more than one night? What are they there for? The staff conference? Some sales training? An illicit adventure? A chance to experiment with their respective gender and sexual identities? And how do they cope with the bathroom situation? The questions are virtually endless...

I keep my door ajar, habitually. Not when I'm staying at hotels, of course, business or otherwise, but when I'm at home or sometimes when I'm staying at a very good friend's house. I like the idea of my bedroom not being closed. It's not as if I was expecting anybody to come and join me in my bed, it's just that I like the idea of the air circulating, and my sleeping self not being entirely confined to a closed room. I also sleep with the window slightly up and the blinds or curtains open. I like seeing a bit of the night time sky as I'm falling asleep, especially if there's a cool moon, and I like being woken up by the rays of the sun alighting on the tip of my nose. I may make an exception to all and any of these behaviours, as and when that seems advisable, which sometimes it is...

At home, my comparatively small bedroom has a very small ensuite bathroom, but I

like that bathroom, because it has an actual
bath in it, and I like to read in the bath. In
fact, I read books almost exclusively in the
bath, because I daren't take my phone or
my laptop to the bath lest I should drop
them, or they should otherwise get wet,
and I hardly ever get around to reading
books anywhere else, since by the time I
usually go to bed I'm too tired to read, and
so I just maybe post a picture of the day to
Instagram or watch a video on YouTube or
Facebook.

I could read on the tube, of course, but
I don't have a daily or otherwise regular
commute, and when I do use the tube I like
to play *Jass* on my app; and when I'm on
a train above ground during the daytime I
like to look out of the window and ponder
the imponderables (such as the conundrum
of the three bed hotel room), or if it is

night time, I'm more likely to be doing some work on my laptop.

In the book I am reading in the bath at the moment, *Becoming a Londoner,* which I'm almost certain my very first boyfriend in London who is now still very good friend gave me relatively recently, the diarist David Plante writes, *"the unintended is truer than the intended."* He in one succinct sentence answers one of the most enduring questions I've had as a writer and as a human being: how is it that I so avoid the plan and favour the detour, that I so value serendipity over completion, that I so relish the random more than I delight in the foreseeable and foreseen? Because they are true. Truer at any rate than anything we think we control. That's why, I'm sure, we all of us, one way or another, seek abandon; gay, or otherwise.

{Felines}

I really like cats.

Maybe that's why I really like men who
behave a little like cats: who come when
they feel like getting some strokes, or some
food, or just like sitting with you on the
sofa, and then for no apparent reason
decide they've had enough now and seek
out their own space and leave you alone to
get on with the day.

It's the opposite of what most people like
from their men: most people seem to like
their men to behave mostly like dogs.

Dogs, with one or two notable
exceptions—one a woolly creature I once
met in the outskirts of Munich and the
other one Harry, a cocker spaniel living

with a family of best friends of mine in the country, who has sadly since been run over by a car—disorientate and bemuse me: their potential for aggression on the one hand and their pathetic neediness on the other disturb me. (Harry, I should point out, seemed to have no potential for aggression. His neediness though was quite pathetic, in a forgivable, canine way.)

Cats don't disturb me. They often make me laugh out loud, and in the main they strike me as abysmally stupid, but when you put an intelligent brain on a cat, say that of a mathematician for example, or a young lifestyle editor, or a social practitioner, then suddenly you have the most perfect pet.

That then begs the question, somewhat, of course: am I primarily after a partner, or am I really after a pet?...

Indiscretion

The man who runs the studio in East London where we're filming has everything he needs to be happy today. A smoothie, the sun, and a freshly cleaned lounger. His is an oasis of rare and extraordinary freedom, and encroaching on it, from all sides, are the capital, the development, the oppressive tentacles of material wealth, and he reckons the days of his haven of creativity are certainly numbered.

'Do you live here?' I ask him.

'Yes,' he says. And then, after a moment's reflection: 'You know, if you're an artist, you have to live differently; otherwise I'd be working for some client now in some graphic design studio.'

He reminds me of me when I was young,
just as young as I was when I was sitting
across from me at the Limonlu Bahçe
in Istanbul. Except he's nowhere near as
young. He's maybe in his late thirties? The
studio at the back of which he has made his
home looks and feels like—and most likely
is—the kind of place that is about to fall
victim to the machine that is stirring right
outside the ramshackle rust-eaten gate:
the ever-encroaching, cold-commercial
boomtown that is spreading out from the
City of London, past Liverpool Street now,
into Shoreditch and beyond.

He keeps the gate locked with a fat
chain and a padlock, 'because it's market
today,' and all manner of people might be
wandering in, some simply curious, some
with ill intent. At lunchtime, as we're
having a break, he unlocks it so those
of us who want to can leave; and in fact

the others all do, while I'm enjoying my moment of peace and quiet in the little courtyard, in the shade. The gate now is shut, but not locked.

A young man with an oddly styled haircut confidently opens the gate, closes it behind himself, and confidently crosses the yard. He has the knack: he has done this before. Confidently, a little cocky, perhaps, he strides to the staircase that's right next to the door that we use for our studio, leading up to the first floor.

Earlier on, our host had shown us a picture of the series he was in the process of taking this afternoon, in his part of the building, at the back. It presented a man completely encased in light beige latex. Not wearing some latex suit or fetish costume, but enclosed in a frame that was covered in latex, from underneath which all the air had been drawn. The man was at the mercy of our host and photographer, completely.

'I could kill him,' he'd said, signalling no intention of doing so. 'It's incredible, the amount of trust.' And it is incredible, the amount of trust that had been placed in his hands by a man who was willing to be trapped in a wrap that could kill him. We'd chatted for quite a while about this and that and the other, when he'd said, 'I better get back, I've left him in there, he's waiting now.'

That was earlier on. Right now, nobody is waiting, but the noticeably confident young man has stridden past me, and our host looks troubled. 'That's not a good sign,' he says, this time only to me, because everybody else has gone out to lunch.

We'd already been made aware that we needed to treat the 'issue' of 'upstairs' with some degree of diligence. 'If there's any issue,' we'd been instructed, 'tell me, and I will go and talk to him,' not specifying who the 'him' in question was.

By that time, I'd only met one person, briefly, and he was sweetness personified: I had just arrived and was not quite yet in the process of setting up, when the door at the top of a short flight of steps inside the building opened, and down came a young man who looked not unlike how you'd imagine Harry Potter, aged 23, minus the scar.

'Do you have a safety pin?' he asked me, which I counted as one of the less conventional opening gambits, but absolutely not without charm. He then proceeded to explain to me in terms almost apologetic that the top button of his shorts had come off, though I didn't quite catch the actual circumstance of this minor calamity. I could not, regrettably, help him with his request, but suggested that our host might have a safety pin for him, with which the young man concurred wholeheartedly, before he disappeared.

The next thing I heard from our host was that there was always the possibility of something of an 'issue' with 'upstairs,' and I naturally assumed that this must entail some ogre, some burly old man, some exceptionally unreasonable or borderline violent landlord; and so I was not a little surprised to learn that the 'issue upstairs' concerned none other than this young, tall and a little gawky guy.

By now I had met him a second time and enquired after his shorts, which he was pleased to inform me had since been mended. Again, I somehow did not quite catch everything that he said; so just how or by whom or when precisely the button had been decalamitised I still didn't know, but I had other things on my mind—such as our impending shoot—and I fancied the delightful chap's shorts were not a matter of sufficient import as to warrant my further attention.

Now, with the arrival of confident lad who had crossed my metaphorical path in a striding fashion, a new layer of possible meanings settled on the situation. He had responded to my 'hello' with a curiously curtailed, so as not to say curt, 'hello,' in which I'd detected neither curiosity nor friendliness, but a perfunctory and, it seemed to me, utilitarian tone that suggested the greeting was there purely because by convention it needed to be, while he, in his stride, cared neither for me nor for the convention. I'd thought not much more of it at that particular moment, because there is only so much significance you assign to a greeting, the greeter's stride not so withstanding, but it had registered as slightly odd—slightly off, to be more precise—and so now it did perturb me just a little that our host so quickly assumed an expression of quite so much concern. 'That is not a good sign,' he said, and I could tell from the way his eyes glanced t'ward the windows upstairs that he meant it. Still I envisioned the ogre, a hideous mountain troll, not the gentle creature with his loose-buttoned shorts, and fully assumed there must therefore be somebody else up there to contend with.

'Why,' I asked, doing my best to sound light of heart, 'is this not a good sign?'
　　　'He's a pusher,' our host explained unequivocally. This meant nothing to me,

which must have shown on my expression,
as it stayed involuntarily blank.

'Do you know what a pusher is?'
'No.'
'He sells drugs.'

My brain now was trying to process the to
me causally unrelated facts that a) there
is an ogre, a cataclysmic Beast of Doom,
living upstairs, who, at any moment, might
turn into an 'issue,' and b) there is a 'pusher,'
somebody who sells drugs, with a strident
gait, who has, for reasons of his own,
now gone up there to that Thing of Terror
and must somehow surely either overcome
or appease it, or succumb to its wrath.

At the same time I was wondering why
our host was calling him a 'pusher' and
not simply a 'dealer.' To me somebody who
comes to your house, or your place of work
or leisure, delivering drugs would be either

a dealer, or somebody acting on behalf of the dealer, such as a courier or delivery person. I had no experience of anyone ever coming around to my house or place of work or leisure delivering drugs, and so I could not be entirely certain, but 'pusher' was a term I would have reserved for somebody who hangs around school yards, for example, and 'pushes' drugs on kids who would not otherwise want them.

But this—the fact that strident fellow was a 'pusher,' whom I would have thought of more as a 'dealer,' was as much of an explanation as was currently forthcoming for the perception, on the part of our host, that the circumstantiality of our shoot at his studio had just acquired an unwelcome layer of anticipated complication, and he said: 'I'll give them half an hour, until quarter past three, and if they're still here then, I'll go and have a word.'

More than anything, what struck me was the grave worry that was written on his face and the sincerity of his concern for our work being able to proceed at all. What there was that might be said to the ogre, who surely by then would have devoured stride-boy, high on the drugs he himself had just delivered, I could not imagine. Certainly, there was nothing I felt I could do, as I had vividly etched on my mind the serious counsel we had been given that we were not to—under any circumstances, as was implied—approach the upstairs den and who or whatever dwelt in it ourselves, but must leave it to our host to deal with any 'issue' that might thence materialise.

My job here today was to direct a delicate scene study, and I had no intention, in any case, to risk life and limb intervening in whatever potential horror might be unfolding upstairs, seeing that it clearly was a situation of its own making. Some people have themselves wrapped in latex and left at the mercy of their kindly and concerned photographer-*cum*-studio-landlord, others obviously deliver (push?) drugs to a mythical menace upstairs from said studio: that's all just Shoreditch on a Sunday in June.

At one point a little later, newly-buttoned-shorts man and the unlikely though strideous 'pusher,' together with somebody I hadn't yet seen or met, but who also didn't strike me as particularly threatening, left the building, the delivery boy—to my mind incongruously—holding two cardboard boxes of a smallish-to-medium size, one under each arm. He looked every bit now the delivery boy, and whatever was in those boxes, I thought, if that's drugs, then you three are going to have yourselves one hell of an afternoon...

Next time I caught the attention of our host, I told him the good news that the 'issue' had, as it appeared, left the building:

'I've seen three of them leave, I think they've locked up.' They had taken pains to put the chain and the lock on the gate upon leaving, which I thought was conscientious and considerate of them. Our host was neither impressed nor convinced. With that ominous glance of his t'ward upstairs, worry weighing on his voice, he said:

'They haven't. They'll have to come back.'

By now, I had me a regular mystery. Since mysteries, regular or not, can only be entertained for so long before curiosity gets the better of their recipient, I now asked him outright what the 'issue' was, with 'upstairs.' Young shorts man, to me, I volunteered, seemed like a thoroughly harmless chap.

'Oh he, is; he's all right. The problem is just that he likes to get high and then get fucked over his desk.' I now had an image in my mind that I was pretty sure didn't belong there and felt that I'd been given more information than strictly I needed to know to continue with this afternoon's proceedings. Then again, I had asked...

It still took me another moment or so to compute why a delightful young man with moderately problematic shorts and a predilection for sex on drugs at his office should be an 'issue' for us, even if it were to happen this afternoon, until the penny dropped, and I realised that the 'issue' in question was simply one of sound intrusion. And maybe a little bit of dust too, because the floor boards of the 'upstairs,' which were old and creaky, were also our ceiling, and we were shooting a dialogue scene of quiet intensity.

They didn't come back. Or maybe they came back later, after we'd already wrapped and gone home. Our sweet-shorted friend may or may not have had his desires met, but there was no 'issue,' that Sunday, for us, from 'upstairs' or elsewhere.

{Closure}

Somebody I speak to at length on a
regular if not particularly frequent basis,
and whose thoughts I greatly respect,
not least because they are more abstract
than any other thoughts I hear routinely
expressed, plays through the possibility
apparently inherent in a Large Hadron
Collider, such as the one operated by
CERN near Geneva, accidentally causing a
mini black hole and thus precipitating and
essentially causing the End of the World.

Instinctively, I consider the likelihood
of this happening minute, but she holds
my gaze a little longer than I expect, and
I read from this that to her mind—and
this is one of the most intelligent minds,
certainly in theoretical matters, I have ever
come across—the probability is not so

remote as to be dismissed lightly, let alone completely.

In a philosophical sense you could argue, and I possibly would, that no probability is so remote as to ever be altogether dismissed, whether lightly or not, but I'm a little startled that of all the people in the world she should contemplate this particular portent so earnestly.

I forget—as I do most things— our conversation momentarily, but then it keeps nudging its way back into my thoughts where, far from frightening or even greatly disturbing me, it fills me with a curiously warm feeling of comfort: If the world should end, I seem to feel (rather than think, because thinking this would to my mind in turn seem counterintuitive and quite irrational), then, no matter how likely or unlikely it may be, the idea of the world ending by a picturesque lakeside near Geneva of all places strikes me as strangely appropriate and beautifully ironic. And, I should say, because of this alone, more probable (if, at this diminutive level of probability, that is still the right word) than almost anywhere else...

Entreatment

I see my Science Communicator Friend next at a party I drag him along to, where we have a long and involved conversation, and where I introduce him to the hosts and to some other people.

It is so easy to talk to him and so comfortable, and he's so easy and comfortable with talking to other people, while I'm distracted talking to other people still, that I begin to formulate in my mind a fantasy that features him and me together. This, I think, is what I would want in a 'boyfriend': somebody I could be so comfortable, so perfectly at ease with, who could hold his own, but, when he didn't need to, would find me interesting enough to converse with me, and who would be interesting enough in his own right to be conversed with, and who had enough going on in his life and thoughts to think and friendships to maintain to be effectively self-sufficient, most of the time, while affectionate and appreciative enough to enjoy some time with me, sometimes.

In retrospect this fantasy grows stronger, not weaker. For a good long while I forget about it, not least because Christmas comes around, and I go to Switzerland, while he has his brother staying over from Greece. Then we see each other once or twice briefly and then not again because he's off to Greece himself. This may or may not have been Easter.

By the time he comes back he has brought me a tea that he has made himself. It's a jar of leaves, and it's my favourite infusion straight away, not just because it's from him, but because it has sage in it, and I love sage. It has one or two other ingredients, maybe three, but I don't now remember what they were. I am touched that he thought of me while away, not least because we're not actually 'together' in any way, we don't even really have sex. One of the first things he'd said, after a bit of what could easily have turned into sex, was: 'let's not get onto sex, it just ruins everything.' And that was all right with me: I found it interesting, but also perhaps true.

Although sex does not, in my experience, have to ruin everything, it certainly can be or become a complicating factor, and several people I'm still excellent friends with I don't think I would still be excellent friends with if we were still having sex, even though I personally tend to think of sex as not much more than a particularly emphatic way of saying 'hello.' I accept that this perception is perhaps not strictly conventional, and I allow for the possibility that I might change it quite drastically too, if I were to actually find myself in a relationship.

We then don't see each other again for a while, this time because I'm away from London for two months while my flat is being renovated, and he's traipsing around Europe, I believe.

By the time we're both back in London, he is enrolled for his MA, whilst I'm not, because I had failed to sufficiently toe the line or impress the course convenor at King's College, London, or both. I am not unhappy about this, though I am of course a bit peeved; but I've since been told, by my Philosopher Friend, that this is not in the least bit surprising since what interests me in philosophy does not, apparently, interest philosophical academia, in fact 'they resent it,' she tells me. I feel reassured by this.

The branch of philosophy that interests me does not yet really exist as a field of academic study, and although I made that clear in my 'submission' to King's (I don't so much like the idea of 'submitting' my work or my thinking to start with, I would consider it more a 'putting it forward,' or 'out there'), they still did not think that either they could offer me anything, or I them. This jarred with me, just a tad, absolutely, not least because I believe that a university course should be open to anyone who wants to take it and fulfils some standard, agreed-upon entry requirements, not to a hand-picked group who already fit an existing institutional mould, but it did not really, in all seriousness, irk me. It would be frivolous to suggest that I had applied for an MA at King's on a whim, but it's also fair to say that I hadn't thought through the implications of studying philosophy at master's level thoroughly.

When I told a good friend from my school days in Switzerland about all this, he looked at me and said, without hesitation: 'Academia is not for you. You're much better off out of it.' I reluctantly concurred, and told him I didn't want to do an MA in philosophy to go into academia but to gain a better grounded understanding of where philosophy stands today. He counselled other avenues to obtain this. I heed his counsel, at least for the time-being...

The fact that my Greek Science Communicator Friend is now doing his MA is neither good news nor bad news as far as I am concerned, it just means he's now back in London, and so am I. I am reminded of him, partly because he gets back in touch and proposes a catchup, and partly because of the book I am reading in the bath at the moment, which my first ex and still very good friend has given to me, *Becoming a Londoner – a Diary*. It's written in an easy-going, relaxed, near conversational prose by a man who had come to London from the United States in his twenties during the early 1960s and quickly started a live-in relationship with a sophisticated Greek man of a similar age, whom he nevertheless appeared to rather revere, if nothing else intellectually.

The diary is rich in anecdotes about the London literary and art world of the day, and although I came to London nearly twenty years later, much of what he writes about, and much of the way he writes about it, resonates with me strongly. Also, he visits places that I have been to, in some cases frequently, such as Lucca, or Paris.

But most enjoyable for me are the insights into the lives of people like Francis Bacon and, most particularly, Stephen Spender, with whom both he and his Greek partner had a close friendship. Each time I read in this book, I am a little reminded of my Greek Science Communicator Friend and of my fantasy of being together with him, which I know full well is all it ever was and ever will be, which is partly what makes it so enjoyable, so safe.

Today, I was hoping to see him for an event at Lights of Soho, which I've recently become a 'member' of. I'd suggested to him that we go there and he'd said, in his usual, non-committal way, that 'this sounds interesting,' but already flagged up the fact that he normally had a seminar at college on a Tuesday and didn't know when this would end. I'd parked the idea, more or less assuming he wouldn't come out with me Tuesday, and indeed, when I sent him a message earlier today, he declined, saying he couldn't get away. I was a little deflated but also quite relieved, since by now I had decided that unless he were to come along, I myself wouldn't go either and had started to hope, almost, that my assumption would prove correct and he wouldn't come out, so I didn't have to go.

Instead, I had a bath and read in my book, which reminded me of him, and then sat down in my white towelling dressing gown, which I hardly ever wear, and when I do then only ever after I've had a bath, and poured myself a glass of white wine and put on an old vinyl record with Eugen Bochum conducting Mozart, and realised that I am very content, almost happy.

I discover a message from him, in response to mine saying not to worry as I was getting too comfortable on my sofa and might not go out myself, in which he says: "Yeah, you should be one with the sofa." And I agree. I am fairly much one with the sofa, right now.

The funniest line so far that I've read in David Plante's book is about Auden, staying with the Spenders: *"Stephen said that once, when Auden was staying at Loudon Road, Natasha rang him up to say she would be late, and would he put the chicken in the oven? Auden did – he simply put it in the oven, didn't put it in a pan, didn't put the heat on."* I so relate to Auden.

{Thoughts That Can't Be Unthunk}

My dad tells me the story of when he, back in 1951, aged eighteen, goes to the Lido on Lake Zürich—where he's grown up and where he has turned himself into a Swiss Youth Champion swimmer—to try out nude bathing.

Being Switzerland and Continental Europe, Zürich has no problem with nude bathing in 1951, and so there is a designated nudist section of the Lido where swimming naked in the Lake may be relished at nature-embracing liberty by anyone so inclined.

"I walked out of the changing rooms, a little shy and uncertain, holding my towel in front of me," I've seen pictures of my dad at that age—not, I hasten to add, in the nude, but wearing his swimming trunks, and in one of them, I believe, his chest adorned with a medal, or so I seem to remember—and my dad as an eighteen year old is exceptionally handsome, he's a youth champion swimmer, after all, "and there were all these saggy old men, with drooping bits everywhere."

I laugh my head off at the thought of my adonis dad walking out into a world full of saggy old men and drooping bits everywhere. They put him right off, so he turned around straight away and never went back, unsurprisingly.

The image, though, lingers...

{Loss}

How grown ups ruin things.

The little boy on the District Line is giddy
with insight, his eyes are aglow with love,
his voice alive with excitement. Swinging
round the pole he's meant to just hold on
to, he tells his friend, 'sometimes I think
that everything is just a dream.' His friend,
just slightly taller, but still little, exclaims:
'so do I!'

It's a moment of sheer wonder. A wonder
dad has lost. Dad says: 'That's the question
my dad likes to think about, how do you
know that everything isn't just a dream;
that we're not in someone's brain...'

The boys try to ignore him, they're not
ready for his existential, inherited angst.

But dad now has the upper hand: 'How do you know,' he insists, 'how do you know you're not dreaming right now?' There's a smile on his face, but it doesn't look as benign as he possibly means it to be: there is power at play now, it's a smirk.

Slightly older but still very young boy has no answer: 'I just know,' he says.

Dad—to the younger boy, they don't look like brothers to me—is like a dog with his bone: 'But how can you be sure? Have you ever had a dream?'

This strikes me as near-cruel a question. These boys are maybe seven, eight? Older, slightly taller, but still nine-years-old-I-imagine-at-the-most boy is now unsure: 'Yes...?' The uncertainty infuses a slight quiver in his voice.

My heart breaks; I want to hug him and
say: 'Everything is all right; and you're
quite right too, and your little friend.
Sometimes everything is just a dream, but
not in this cynical, clinical way your little
friend's dad now makes you think and
worry about.' Still dad won't let go and
instead pushes on with his inquisition,
until: 'You start freaking me out,' the little
boy says.

At last dad relents, sensing the fear he
has just poured over his son and his son's
gschpänli, who were just a moment ago
so excited that everything could still be a
dream, and to whom until just a moment
ago it probably was...

The tear I shed for these boys is as
heavy as the joy was light that I felt for
their innocence. If only dad had had a
wiser father. The prism of your childhood

paints the world in colours that but slowly fade, and if it is tainted, obscured or damaged, oh how long a shadow it casts...

Whist

'My girlfriend is getting texty,' the man who ticks every box and makes me go aglow inside tells me. He's a trombonist, and that alone should tell me everything I need to know. Except he's also tall and blond and a bit Scandinavian looking and exceptionally friendly, and he has that borderline cute proportion of a long torso and comparatively short legs that make him just simply adorable.

I have nothing to say about this. Therein lies the 'interesting' realisation. It's 'interesting' in so far as I normally have something to say about things. I pride myself—not 'pride myself' so much as find a certain degree of satisfaction that I try not to let seep into smugness if I can possibly help it, though sometimes I think

in this I fail—in being able to find words.
I like words, I love—nay, *relish!*—them.
I use more words than necessary. What
is necessary? I get admonished for being
verbose. What, pray, is verbose? I say things
for the sake of saying them. Thrice. I use
language people don't understand, but I get
tasked with making things understandable,
as a job. I like that. I like ironies, I like
perplexities, I like conundrums and calling
them conundra. I have said so before, but
I like to say things again. I like repetition.
Repetition. There you go: I like it.
Repetition.

In the Game of Love & Chance—I like
ampersands! And I love interjections, or
little asides...—I am particularly useless,
but I have of late started to enjoy that
fact, rather than despair over it. It used
to trouble me. Astonishing men like my
Trombonist Friend right here and right

now used to send me down a spiral of
remorse and regret, about what I knew not.

About not having loved. About not
having lived. About not having taken the
chance. Now that I've taken the chance
once or twice and then thrice and several
times more, and notwithstanding the fact
that this has sometimes but certainly not
always paid off, and now that I realise that
a 'girlfriend getting texty' is just exactly
the kind of thing that would drive me
up the wall, even if it were a boyfriend as
handsome and delectable as her boyfriend
right now, I can smile at the man's beauty
and charm and listen to the resonance
of his torso and admire the sounds he
produces from his instrument and say to
myself: that has nothing whatever to do
with me. It's wonderful, and wonderful for
him too. And I wish him really, and
genuinely, well.

I love that kind of love. It's taken me maybe
thirty-five years—five heptades!—to get
to this point, but I'm now at a point where
I can absolutely love a man like that and
know his life has absolutely nothing to do
with me beyond the set of fortuitousnesses
that brought us together in this context,
at this moment, for this short period, and
then let that be as it may. And should our
paths cross again, then so much the better,
but it would still not mean anything else
or anything more or anything less. And
should we become friends through our
paths crossing further, that too would be
just that, and it would be just fine. My
Trombonist Friend shows me that I am all
right. He is marvellous, in my mind; and
let that forever be so: I am perfectly all
right with that too.

We part and go our separate ways, and I
think of it or of him no more, and I am
where I once was and where for a long time
I longed to be anew: unencumbered and
free. I use these words a lot, I now find, it
must mean they have become important to
me.

I see on the social network that he's doing
something exciting with his trombone
and his musician friends and the band
somewhere, and I am deeply happy and
unreasonably proud. I have no cause and
no reason to be proud, I have nothing
to do with his or any of his colleagues'
achievements, but I still feel a little proud
of him and of them, as if it had something
to do with me. And maybe it does have
something to do with me, in as much as
I know him, and we've once tangentially
worked together (worked on the same
piece, at least, for a very short while),

and so at least in as much as everything
is connected, and this therefore perhaps
really also connects us a little, it may have
a tiny little something to do with me, and
that thought alone makes me happier still.

And now the words are there, and they are
no better and no worse than any other, and
that too is just fine and dandy. All words
need not be weighty and grave. Some could
do with being a bit more poetic probably
than they are, but mostly they merely need
to ring true. And this, to me, if nothing
else, is true.

{Mystery}

I wake up wondering once again, as so
often, how the little horse got on the boat
in the first place, let alone why it voyaged
so far: who let it on, was there no-one to
lead it off, by its halter, for example, back
onto dry land, to its own pastures, that
were maybe not so green, but familiar,
at least? Why was it by the pier, near the
harbour even? I suppose horses do live by
the seaside, it is not unheard of, but it vexes
me. A horse belongs onshore, as far as I'm
concerned, in my inexpertise.

I try to think this through and come up
with several potential scenarios, none of
which satisfies as an explanation. Perhaps
the little horse accidentally strayed onto
a cargo ship and was mistaken there for

one of the ones that were actually being
exported, by coincidence, just then. Maybe
it wasn't so much a coincidence, maybe the
horse got friendly with, even enamoured
of, one of the horses that—very possibly
against their own will or better instinct—
were being embarked right now and just
followed it, in equine loyalty and affection.

Perhaps it was being sold: it could simply
be that it was 'mine'—as in the person
writing the song, thus narrating the story
and lamenting the absence of 'my' little
horse, wishing it back—only by extension,
and really it belonged to the family or to
my father, and he, for reasons best known
to him (but there are many imaginable:
economic hardship, disaffection with
the beast, or having gambled it away to a
foreign sailor, notwithstanding the riddle
as to what a sailor, of all people, would
do with a pony – maybe sell it on?...),

had exchanged it for goods or money, or forfeited it; and now, as I sit here on my own watching the waves roll in from afar, it has long since sailed away, right over the ocean, over the sea.

Then suddenly it hits me, out of the blue. It has all been a misunderstanding. Where I went to school, in Basel, we had an annual 'bazar.' I can't be sure any more was it at this bazar, which everybody pronounced *baht*zar,' and which happened a few weeks before Christmas to raise funds for the school, or was it at the summer fete, which happened every year in the summer, probably just before the big holidays, to the same end, or both, but there was a little patch of wood in the school grounds where sometimes, not always, some generous soul would bring along a couple of ponies, so the children could go pony riding for a franc or two. This was almost

the only occasion that ever presented itself
to me to see, or think of, or hear about,
ponies. Even though they spelt 'Pony' the
same as in English, just with a capital for
being a noun, everybody called a pony *'es
Bonny,'* pronouncing it with an at best half
committed P and without the prerequisite
diphthong, making it sound exactly like
'Bonnie.' For years—*years!*—I would stand
in class amongst my *gschpänlis* and intone
with devotion a plea for someone, anyone
really, to bring back, bring back, oh bring
back my little horse to me. And for years—
years!—I could not fathom why the little
horse had ever gone away, there just seemed
to be no plausible explanation for this. And
now—*now!*—it turns out there didn't ever
need to be.

At last, one of the great bewildering
conundrums of my childhood
simply, quietly, evaporates...

Perfection

That day the universe was on my side. Because for the first time ever it gave me not just a second chance, but a third; and that really had never happened before. I never even normally get the second chance, for the simple and obvious reason that it's just very unlikely to come about, so to be given a third chance – imagine how lucky I felt, and how happy.

I was on my way to the party; that was on Monday. I was in a good frame of mind, I had just arrived in town and seen two decent films, and I'd picked up my invitation and now was determined to go to this party even though I knew nobody there, and I thought I might therefore leave it again very soon. But in my good frame of mind I started chatting to a woman

on the shuttle bus that the festival laid
on from the last screening in the grand
piazza to the lido by the lake where the
party was happening, and after seeming a
little distant at first she then, as we arrived
there, almost grabbed my hand, and we
went to the bar and had our first few drinks
together, talking a lot about this, that and
the other, and I thought this is great: I'm
already not alone at the party.

When she left, I spotted a good looking
man with a beard who was on his own and,
buoyed by my success so far, started talking
to him, and for a while we had more
drinks and chatted about this and that too
(though not so much about the other), and
he met some people he knew, and I talked
to them as well, and I quite liked him,
but I also realised he probably wasn't that
interested in me, and that was fine by me
too.

We'd by now drifted back towards the bar, and then suddenly out of nowhere the handsomest, friendliest, loveliest of all the men at the party—and it was a fairly big party—stood next to me and looked me in the eyes, and we hugged, and we kissed, and I don't know why that happened so quickly or how, I only know that I'd seen him before, when he was working, taking pictures, and he had pointed his camera at me and the woman from the shuttle bus, and I had raised my glass to him and said 'cheers,' and now here he was, and we were kissing and hugging, and I didn't know how or why: we must have been into each other, I suppose.

It was now nearing the end of the party, coming up four in the morning, and people were already leaving, and he simply said, 'so to Locarno?' and I said, 'yes;' and on the

way to the car he told me he was staying
in a flat with ten people in it, and some of
them needed a lift, so we may have to wait
for them, and I said that was all right, but
in the end nobody wanted a lift—those
who were there at the party decided to
go by other means, maybe walk, or by
bicycle—so we took his car, a convertible,
though he didn't put the roof down, maybe
because it was coming up four o'clock in
the morning. He told me he didn't have his
licence at the moment, but that that was all
right, and I thought, well, he'll be driving
carefully then, and he did, and we got there
without problem, but with a little help
from his phone.

As we entered the flat it was dark and
already quiet, and in the darkness we
walked through a room with nothing much
and nobody in it (maybe it was a hall?),
into another room, which had a large

double bed with two people in it, a man and a woman, both young, maybe the same age as he, and there was a narrow mattress on the floor, and he said: 'this is me, but it's all right,' and it was all right.

We lay down on his little bed, and within seconds we were undressed and were what used to be called making love, and it felt like that, it felt like we were just making some love, and the couple in the bed did not seem to notice or mind and then we both fell asleep in each other's arms.

Now and then the man from the bed would call my young lover's name because he was snoring, and that wouldn't help, so I would hug him closer to me, and that would.
In the morning we woke up, and he said: *'dormi* – sleep,' but he had to get up and go to work, and I got up too though I didn't strictly have to go to work, but I did have

to go to the flat where I was staying, and do some work there. He made me a coffee, and we kissed again and hugged and said goodbye, and he disappeared, I assumed into the shower.

I got dressed in the room with the big double bed and the little single mattress, and a young woman there was also getting dressed, and I left my card on the window sill and let myself out and walked home in the happy sunshine.

He didn't phone me or text me, or send me an email, or friend me on Facebook, and I thought, well that's fair enough, he'd told me how much work he's got on during the festival here, and he was young, so maybe that was just that, and that's fair enough. But a little part of me wished and hoped and believed I would see him again; I would bump into him, I reckoned, at some point during the festival, it's not that big a town, after all.

Nothing happened till Friday, except I was happy all week, doing some work and watching some films, and then Friday I was out with some friends, and we'd just had something to eat and decided to get an ice cream before watching a late film together, and from the ice cream stand I could see him walk towards the Piazza Grande, and I thought there he is, but he didn't spot me, and I was too far away to call him over, and I didn't know whether he'd want me to call him over since he hadn't called me, and he was gone, and I thought, ah well, that's a pity, but maybe there will be a second chance (even though I don't normally get a second chance, as most people don't, most of the time: the probability of circumstances arranging themselves such

that one could come about being just so
incredibly small).

Once everyone had their ice cream, we
realised we were running late for the film,
so we started to make a move towards the
cinema, and there he was again, coming my
way now, with a plate of food in his hand
and passing at just a couple of feet distance:
again I didn't call him or stop him or say
hello, it happened too quickly, we were
late for our film, he had his hands full with
food, and he didn't see me, again. And
again I thought, ah what a pity, but maybe
there will be a third chance, even though
I had never had a third chance before, or
heard of anybody who had.

We went to see the film, and then on the
way back we passed a bar with a big garden
where sometimes they play live music, and
one of the group said let's not go in here,

there's another one which is nicer, but
the other place was already closed, so we
returned to the one with the big garden,
and it's a huge garden with different
sections separated by old stone walls on
different levels, and it would be impossible
to get a view of it all, especially at night
when it isn't that brightly lit, and usually
very busy, and we were going to stand in
the courtyard nearest the bar, but then the
same member of the group said, let's go
up there, and we went up a flight of steps,
past another bar, and into another little
courtyard, and we sat down at a table, and
no sooner had we sat down at the table
than I saw the back of the head that I
recognised.

He was on the phone, stroking his short
bleached hair with his free hand, and I
recognised his short bleached hair in an
instant, as I had stroked it too and so much

liked the feel of it against the palm of my hand, and I recognised the little wrist band that looked like it had come from another festival, probably music, and I thought I should get up now and say hello to him, but he was with a group of people and so was I, and I thought, ah well, he's here and at one point I'll get up and say hello or he'll get up and turn around; and then he finished his conversation on the phone and got up and turned around and there he was.

I said his name, and he said: 'Sebastian.' And we hugged and gave each other a kiss, and he told me he had a problem with his flat which he needed to sort, but how long was I here for now and what had happened to me Tuesday morning, and I told him I'd left him a card and didn't want to hang around as I knew he would have to go to work, and he said he hadn't seen the card but now that he knew where it was he would find it, but I gave him another one 'just in case,' and he looked glad to see me, and we held each other's hands, and we hugged again and gave each other another kiss, and then he had to go and sort his problem with the flat; and I knew that the universe had been kind to me, because it had given me not just a second chance but a third, and I had taken not the first, not the second, but the third chance, and I don't know if we will see each other ever again, but just knowing that he was glad to see me again now, and to see that spark in his eye and feel that hair and hear him say 'Sebastian' and smiling at me his broadest of smiles, that alone completely made me happy that day.

Success

The young man I'm on a date with is really unbearably cute. 'You're really unbearably cute,' I tell him. 'I know,' he says, with the smile of someone who really does, and an involuntary shrug: 'I try. I succeed.'

It's happy hour at the Troubadour, my favourite haunt and quasi home from home, and so I look forward to an early evening mojito. This, here at the Troubadour, is contingent upon the other person also wanting a mojito. Or at any rate the same cocktail: you get two for one, but only as long as they're the same drink. Why, is a mystery to me, but not one that has ever bothered me enough to prompt me to enquire about its reason: it's rarely a problem, since I've come across few people in my life who don't like a mojito, and for those who don't, there's always the option of a Bloody Mary. Or any other standard you'd expect on a short but traditional menu. I worry not.

Robert, the friendly and forever charming and helpful waiter appears, and as I propose this to start the evening by way of an almost foregone conclusion, my young and very new friend throws an unexpected spanner in the works: 'I don't drink alcohol.'

'What, not at all?'

'No, I used to, but I didn't really like it, and I got too drunk a couple of times, so I've stopped altogether, but you go ahead.'

'Are you sure?'

This is dodgy territory. If I drink and he doesn't, doesn't this unbalance our universe—in which, at least for the next few hours, we are meant and agreed to proceed together—and not necessarily in anyone's favour? I'm concerned now that this date may not go so well after all...

'Yes absolutely, I really don't mind. Seriously.'

His smile remains confident and sincere, and so I turn to Robert who is waiting on us, patient and knowing, while this short negotiation takes place, and I order the mojito nonetheless. Robert, bless him, reads the situation just fine and innocently asks if I want the happy hour anyway. I'm stumped once again, but before I can say anything more my young friend says, 'sure, go ahead;' and so it comes to pass that I'm on a date with an unbearably cute young man who doesn't drink at all, while I'm being brought two mojitos by Robert, who does not bat an eyelid.

They look incongruous on the table in front of me, these mojitos, next to his elderflower cordial, but just for about the first five minutes or so. Soon I ease into the conversation, and I bask in the glow of a man who is so comfortable with everything and with himself that I feel this is perfectly all right, I can enjoy this, I can relax…

Trivia

The world, I realise with a pang of melancholy and nostalgia, has become a slightly more prosaic, pragmatic, perfunctory place while I was away.

I was away in Brazil for two months (and stories entirely of their own kind and wonder were lived and experienced there, which to regale you with is for another place and another time, for certain), and since I had set off to São Paulo from Zürich, I flew back to Zürich for a few more days in Switzerland with my family before taking a plane home to London, only to find on that particular flight that the world had, in these few weeks, been impoverished and made just that bit more mundane.

I knew this was going to happen, yet it still came as a shock to the system. A trivial, first-world-problem kind of shock, no doubt, but still: British Airways had ditched the 'free' drinks—the drinks were never really 'free;' they were included and obviously somehow accounted for in the airfare—and now sent its little trolley down the aisle, charging you for every last peanut off it.

In theory, that is. In practice, this newly utilitarian procedure, which now involved taking card payments from everybody for every coffee and every water, let alone every little bottle of wine, every can of beer, and every snack, took so long that by the time they got to me in row 21, the announcement came through that we now needed to fold up our tables and put our seat backs in the upright position, because we were just about to touch down in Heathrow.

There may well be a commercial argument for not including drinks on short haul routes that other providers offer at rock bottom prices, and the 'free snacks' had long dwindled to such minuscule sampler sachets of some desolatory crackers or crisps that in fact the idea of suddenly now being able to choose from a whole range of sandwiches, wraps and porridges sounded like a genuine improvement. In theory, once again, that is. In practice, any hope of obtaining any actual food was foiled by the reality that by the time they got to me in row 21, they were not only out of time, but they had sold out of everything edible on their trolley, and so, even if there had been enough of a flight left to eat something (which there wasn't), there was nothing now on offer to buy.

But whether any of this makes sense commercially, or simply reflects the harsh reality of a fiercely competitive market, racing itself to the unforgiving bottom of absolute discomfort in a fight for dubiously worthwhile survival amidst the ruthless cannibalism of 'no-frills,' 'no-standards,' 'no-pleasure' operators run by crude Irishmen, what pains the heart and saddens the soul is the realisation that the poetry of flying, such as it, barely, still was, and had, even at this most basic level, been cultivated, still, a little at least, by BA, has now been wiped out by brute rationality.

I so fondly remember a flight to Nice— not that long ago—where I found myself sitting next to an improbably well spoken and strikingly beautiful woman who was also on her way to the film festival in Cannes, and who, witnessing me order a

Bloody Mary and realising that that was just part of the service provided by British Airways, decided with enthusiasm that that was exactly what she wanted too.

We naturally got talking, and roughly a quarter into our conversation we were nearly out of Marys. This looming crisis was noted by the attentive cabin crew, who immediately offered us each another. Halfway through our conversation we obviously needed a third one, which, in truth, we this time had to ask for, but which we were served with unflinching, even indulgent, patience and a smile by our delightful flight attendant. And whether or not, for the last quarter of our conversation, we required, requested and were given our fourth Bloody Mary, I can't now with certainty recall, mostly because we were really quite jolly by then (in the most agreeable way), and it was, after all, still mid-morning, but I certainly like to think so.

And the beauty of it: that was all there ever was to it. We never kept in touch, we never met up, and, although she was bound to have told me, I have no idea what she was doing in Cannes. We didn't even exchange details. Once, on another flight back from Nice to London I actually ended up involved in some potentially useful networking; on this occasion, though, no purpose whatever was served: we just had ourselves a wonderful flight and positioned ourselves in a perfect frame of mind for the festival, thanks entirely to BA.

But now, when you fly with BA to Nice to attend the film festival in Cannes, it will feel just like any other airline, and not much different to a National Express coach or an East Coast Line train to Leeds. You can buy yourself a vodka and a tomato juice, of course, and if you're extremely lucky, they may even find you a slice of lemon. They won't have the Worcester sauce for you though, and although it will taste bland but still cost you nearly as much as a legendary Bloody Mary at the Century Club, it is possible, just, that economically you actually fare better with one or two like this that you pay for, than you would if their potential cost had been factored into the price of your ticket.

And true: if you went for three or four drinks with mixers, as we did, it's likely that a fellow passenger who was just drinking water was subsidising you, in those days. Yet, isn't that the kind of thing that makes life worth living? That sometimes you find yourself in a situation where in all likelihood you're indirectly buying a drink for someone you've never met, and other times you become the recipient, quite unexpectedly, of such similar munificence, because in a civilised society having a Bloody Mary is considered par for the course on an aeroplane? And on that rare and exquisite occasion when you sit next to a person so articulate and so beautiful that this one Bloody Mary just turns into four, well then so be it?

That way, surely, lies the generosity of gesture that makes it all bearable; and the moment, surely, will come—I daresay it has most certainly occurred many times before—when someone on a plane who paid just the same as I did has something to celebrate and gets bumped up and offered a glass of champagne, or when somebody somewhere in some other context is inadvertently, involuntarily, yet graciously, still, my guest.

I welcome them to it and wish them well.
And I wish BA would rethink their mean-
spirited approach, and not just for my
sake, or the sake of my fellow passengers.
I recently had a long conversation with
a man who works as cabin crew for BA.
And oh how unhappy he did sound.
How demoralised. How sad. About the
state of affairs. About the cost-cutting
culture. About the dwindling levels of
service he is able, even encouraged, to
provide. About the erosion of anything
resembling an ethos. About the way in
which being BA—just as flying BA—
feels no longer special, but has become
pedestrian, mercenary, banal. And there,
precisely, lies the beginning of the end of
civilisation: when what matters is no longer
the sophistication of your experience, the
excellence of who you are and what you
stand for, and the pride and joy you take
and make from and through what you do,

but purely the profit, and nothing else.
What a poor world we live in, where only
the profit matters, and nothing else.

It may only be, on the surface, about
a complimentary Bloody Mary. On
reflection, it turns out to be far from trivial,
after all...

{Irk}

The elderly lady with silver grey hair and
a formidable bosom corners the festival's
Programming Director and demands that
he explain himself.

Her hair is tied at the back in an elegant
bow, and her glasses suggest literacy
both cinematic and literary. Her lips are
glossed red, but the upper lip is quite thin,
and the lower lip is quite full, and at the
corners these lips pull somewhat towards
eighteen past eight, which gives her a
permanent expression of ever so marginally
lopsided vexation. She bears an uncanny
resemblance to Mrs Richards who pitches
up in Episode One of the second series of
Fawlty Towers, but this lady is not unhappy
with her view, nor is she hard of hearing;

she hears all too well, and what she objects to is English.

What irks—so as not to say angers—her ('anger' seems too uncouth a term for her form of displeasure) is that here in Locarno, the picturesque lakeside town with the second oldest international film festival in the world after Venice, an announcement (or was it a speech? I am not entirely sure now) was made not in Italian (the language of the Canton Ticino, where we find ourselves), or any of the other official languages of Switzerland, German, French or Rumantsch, but in the language of the global village, English.

She had no problem understanding it—she probably has a Swiss education, and her English is likely to be better than that of two thirds of all native English speakers around the world—her objection is one of principle. One of culture, even. And a concern for how what is being cultivated—the unstoppable advance of the current *lingua franca* (obviously, and as the term itself reminds us, not the first one to sweep the globe, and it won't be the last)—on the multilingual diversity of parochial Europe, specifically Switzerland.

This diversity has real charm, and, when witnessed in action, can be seriously impressive. It's not just the trains here which routinely make all major announcements in three languages (one of which is always English, although English is not an official language in Switzerland), or the packaging of consumer goods, which mostly (but not always) eschews English but finds room, on such everyday produce as butter and milk, for all four national languages; it's when you see and hear people actually using their languages seamlessly and matter-of-factly across their spectrum that you realise how capable we can be if we try.

Not long before this 'incident' in Locarno, I'd been to the other major film festival in Switzerland, Solothurn. This, unlike Locarno, is not an international affair but focuses entirely on Swiss film making; it is therefore not of global significance, but really important to Switzerland. A close friend of mine had directed the opening film. He'd also fallen out with his erstwhile best friend, who was the producer, over it, and so it was this not an entirely happy occasion. It was nonetheless memorable, not least for the opening speeches. I don't remember their exact sequence, but: one was held by the then Artistic Director of the festival, who happened to be from the Ticino and therefore spoke in Italian. One was held by the then

President of the Federal Council (this, in the egalitarian direct democracy that is Switzerland is a nominal role rotating on an annual basis through the Federal Council, which consists of seven members who are elected by parliament and who form the government of the country as a joint cabinet; the President of Switzerland therefore only ever is in office for one year as a *primus inter pares),* who happened to be French speaking and therefore gave her address in French. And a third was held by some dignitary from the Swiss film making community, who spoke German. There were no translations, no subtitles, no surtitles, no captions. The expectation was—as it is in the chambers of the national parliament—that everyone in the audience (which here, this being an open event, is the general public) speaks at least two, but preferably three, of the four national languages. And they do. Mostly.

But you are talking about a film-festival-going audience with a particular interest in Swiss films. You are talking about Solothurn, not Locarno.

Locarno is one of the most important and quite possibly the most beautiful film festival for independent film in the world, and so obviously not everybody attending it speaks either Italian, or German, or French, or let alone Rumantsch. (Hardly anybody in Switzerland speaks Rumantsch: it has a native speaker base of some 36,000 individuals with about another 25,000 people speaking it 'regularly.' It's a lovely language, though, and not at all impossible to learn, especially if you have Latin.)

The irony for my Swiss Mrs Richards in particular, and for us all, is that the one language almost all Swiss people speak to at least basic level—many to near perfection—is English. Professors often lecture in English at universities, there are kindergartens and pre-school groups conducted in English (also in Putonghua, now, as it happens), and it is not unheard of for high school students to deliver their papers in English. And with so many people living and working and travelling in Switzerland from all over the world, the one language you know for certain you'll get by in is, of course, English.

The festival's Programming Director is patient and polite. He gives a somewhat resigned looking smile—resigned more, I think, to the fact that being accosted with these kinds of grievances is simply part of the job, even if he's really just here tonight outside this cinema to see a film at his festival, than resigned to the realities of globalisation—and explains the situation to his questioner in her

seventies not unlike you would to a child
of about seven. I half fear me she may feel
patronised. She doesn't. Her eyes light up,
and she feels taken seriously. Her lips, at
first reluctantly, but then giving themselves
over to reconciliation, flatten out into
almost a smile of her own. I wonder has
he just charmed her. He is very charming,
in a slightly headmasterly way: the kind of
person who daily has to deal with unruly
students and their impossible parents alike,
and who just takes it all in his steady, slow-
paced, long-suffering stride.

My queue starts to move, and I lose track
of them both and their conversation. I
don't think it was his perfectly reasonable
argument that won her over, I think it
was just that he managed to signal to her
for three minutes or four that he cared for
her irk. And I'm almost certain he did, for

three or four minutes. Which is probably about as much as it merited, after all. What the film was that I saw, or what language it was in, or how it was subtitled (all films at these festivals are always subtitled), I can't recall, but the introduction, I'm almost certain, was given in English…

Shea

Shea works in my local Sainsbury Local, and I don't know him at all. I like him enormously. He is tall, lanky, probably in his mid-twenties, and he has the confidence of an old hand. He calls all his male customers 'mate' and all his female customers 'darling,' and he takes excellent care while packing the bags to stack the stuff I buy in them sensibly. The first time I witness him in action I don't talk to him beyond the 'hello' and 'thank you' that get you through checking out, but I'm fascinated by his quiet concentration and diligence that he combines with an unalloyed pride in, and joy for, what he is doing. His long-armed gestures are almost those of a conductor who here does not conjure notes from a band of musicians, but directs these goods from their basket where they need to go in my bag, precisely.

On my next visit to the store, he's wearing a name badge on which it says 'Khalid.' This is the first and so far only time that I talk to him. I say: 'Last time I saw you, you were called "Shea."' He laughs. 'Yes,' he says, 'I've lost my name badge. The other day I was "Matt," but really I'm Shea.' This makes me like him even more. Shea is Shea, whether the label says Matt, Khalid or Shea, it really doesn't matter to him. It doesn't matter to me.

There's also a very beautiful and very polite young woman at the same little store who asks me how the writing is going each time she sees me. The exchanges over the few minutes it takes to process a basket of groceries are never profound, but they are profoundly meaningful nonetheless, at that simple, non-directional, subtly subconscious and superficially purposeless level where someone with a utilitarian mindset and an eye on efficiency would argue the interaction isn't even necessary: 'It's functionally superfluous, a machine can do what these people do, why do we pay them a wage?'

Next to the tills there's a small bank of self-service checkout machines that talk at you. I loathe them. I am no technophobe, in fact the opposite: I embrace technology and think much of it marvellous, and I practically live online. Self-service checkouts with their rigid, robotic, soulless adherence to a stubborn protocol, their loud, unmodulated, miscalibrated tone, and their inability to conclude more than one in three procedures without the intervention of one of their human helpers infuriate and offend me.

Occasionally, when there's a long queue for the tills and I have only a few items, I use them, reluctantly, grudgingly, they way you succumb to the Borg. They may be practical and save you a few minutes, if all goes well, but in civilisatory terms they are an abomination.

A while ago there was a woman called Rose, at the same store. She told me she loved travel, and it transpired she used to be a doctor. She was in her sixties, maybe; well-spoken and dignified. She'd taken the job to get out of the house, to have some human contact, she didn't really need the money, she just wanted to do something rather than sit at home and read. As I watch Shea take a bottle of Pinot Grigio from my basket, handle it like an object of personal value, remove its security contraption as you would take the hat off a child, and carefully place the bottle in

a carrier bag, just in the right position so
it won't crush the apples or tilt over the
falafel, having put aside the eggs and the
salad, of course, because they obviously
need to go on top of the yoghurts, I feel
me a great glow of love for him. And for
Rose. And for the young woman whose
name I still haven't learnt, though she
remembers that I'm a writer. And for the
middle-aged lady at my local Waitrose,
who greets me like a long lost friend when,
having been away for a while, I return
to her till. And the young man there too
who had to tape up his earlobe with a
ridiculous blue bandaid because the store
manager made him take out his stretch
ring, which rendered his ear so much more
conspicuous than if he'd just been allowed
to wear the ring, but who carried himself,
and carried on with his job, in the finest
of spirits, because that's just the kind of
pettiness you have to put up with when

you're a little extraordinary, now and then;
and the young woman who greets me
with an indulgent smile to this day when
she sees me, because one early morning,
several years ago, having partied rather too
hard through the night, I came to her till
a little the worse for wear trying to buy a
bunch of 'personal items' only to realise
I didn't even have my wallet on me… I'm
not friends with any of them. I don't feel
that I need to be either. I just need them to
be there and to remind me, every so often,
how beautiful humans are, even when they
perform the apparently simplest of tasks.
You can rationalise away the transaction,
but you're a long way from making me love
the machine.

I salute you, Shea, and all your wondrous
colleagues: you make this world a little
more worth living in, indeed.

{Coda}

It is the eyes
I realise
when looking
as I do
when searching
(as I want not to but need)
for something that says
yes?
perhaps inflected as a question, as
a thought, a hesitancy only
not as affirmation
or commitment, as
an option to
connect –

A possibility of tendernesses
be they real, imaginary or
relived as confirmation, as some
memories

of things to come, I give them
equal weightlessness, they are
but temporary, filigree
they may not be
the substance
or the solid core
the scaffold or the frame
on which the edifice of life is built
yet they are delicate
refined
exquisite
joyful
brief
but lasting
in their value
in their glow.

I cannot take my eyes off you
no matter who you are, I see in you
the multitudes of selves reflected that I love
I need you not
to be mine

or to tell me
that I'm dear to you, or let alone
unique
I need you only to
smile back at me
and let those windows to your soul say
maybe: maybe.

Maybe that which you are looking for
that which you see in me
that which you never thought of to declare
but daily yearn to live
to give and to receive
that which you know though you may not
have words for it
that which you never knew but always
knew would one day find you
that which is you, that
which is you
may yet, may: just
may, yet
be